Hísientina houn niduheñu. Haríenga nun,
"Durati bau, Chuti bau."
"Walagante" lian háwaru nun ladüga tonwe núguchu.
My mother's relatives loved me. They said,
"You are so smart. You have great understanding."
They called me, "Walagante" which means "our legacy", the legacy of my mother who had died.

Marcella Lewis
Sunrise January 20, 1920
Sunset July 22, 2006

Other Books in Garifuna:

The People's Garifuna Dictionary: Dimureiágei Garifuna. Garifuna - Inglesi, English - Garifuna. National Garifuna Council of Belize, 1993, Reprinted 2005.

Hernandez, Felicia, 1993. *Narenga: A Garifuna Children's Book.* New York: Chanti Publications

Arana, Pietra, 1993. *Lemesi Lidan Garifuna: The Garifuna Mass.* Belize: Benex Press

Castillo, Jesse, 1992. *Garifuna Folk Tales*

A BILINGUAL BOOK:
GARIFUNA/ENGLISH

Walagante Marcella
Marcella Our Legacy

Poetry and Other Writings
by Marcella Lewis

Foreword by Sebastian and Fabian Cayetano

Edited by Judy Lumb and Roy Cayetano

Illustrated by Judy Lumb

National Garifuna Council
Producciones de la Hamaca
Caye Caulker, BELIZE

Copyright ©1994 Marcella Flores Lewis
Reprinted 2010

All rights reserved under International Copyright Conventions.

Published for the National Garifuna Council by *Producciones de la Hamaca,* Caye Caulker, Belize

ISBN 978-976-8142-00-9

The mission of the National Garifuna Council is to advocate for and secure the rights, development, and culture of the Garifuna in Belize, while promoting economic sustainability, interracial harmony and maintaining traditional respect for the preservation of the environment.

Producciones de la hamaca is dedicated to:

- Celebration and documentation of Belize's rich, diverse cultural heritage,
- Protection and sustainable use of Belize's remarkable natural resources,
- Inspired, creative expression of Belize's spiritual depth.

Contents

Foreword ... 1

POEMS

Garinagu Sarawama: Chülüha Dan	2
Garinagu Arise: The Time Has Come	3
Nageira	4
My Home	5

AUTOBIOGRAPHY

Núragate	6
My Story	7

POEMS

Yalifu	14
Pelican	15
Lubuidu Láfuaru Hati	16
How Beautiful the Moonrise	17
Lubuidu Láfuaru Weyu Binafi	18
How Beautiful the Sunrise	19
Wéyasu	22
Journey	23
Béibuga Luma Inarüni	24
Walk With Truth	25
Hísienti Nageira Nun	26
Hísienti Sawanah Nun (Uremu)	26
I Love My Home (Poem)	27
I Love The Savanna (Song)	27
Duna Churunruti Dangriga	28
Stann Creek River	29
Kalifónia	30
California	31

STORY

Áfaraha Ta Garadun Mesu	34
The Mouse Beat the Cat	35

SPEECH

Uguñe Haweyuri Sun Úguchu	36
Today we Honor All Mothers	37

SONGS

Lubuidu Namule Eyeri	38
My Pretty Baby Brother	39
Keimoun Numa	40
Come with me	41
Mábuiga María	42
Lúguchu Wabureme	42
Hail Mary	43
Mother of Our Savior	43
Wáguchu Gúnfulitu	44
Úguchuru Arufudabawa	44
Our Holy Mother	45
Mother Show Us	45
Hilatibu Luagu Gurúa Wawagu Wáguchi	46
You Died on the Cross for Us	47
Saraya Bungiu	48
God Has Risen	49
Sian Béheraha Tuma	50
Duña Duña Dun	50
You Cannot Laugh	51
Pepe Catches a Fish	51

MUSIC

Buíti Binafi	52
One Day Tiofila Gone By the Well	54
Keimoun Numa	55
Hísienti Sawana Nun	56

Mábuiga María	58
Lúguchu Wabureme	59
Wáguchu Gúnfulitu	60
Úguchuru Arufudabawa	61
Hilatibu Luagu Gurúa Wawagu Wáguchi	62
Saraya Bungiu	64
Lubuidu Namule Eyeri	66
Sian Béheraha Tuma	67
Duña Duña Dun	68

Editor's Notes:
For Those Unfamiliar with the Garifuna Language	69
Bibliography	74

FOREWORD

Mrs. Marcella Lewis is an outstanding woman and a legendary figure among Garinagu throughout Belize. She has made an immense contribution to the cultural and literary development of Garinagu and Belize. In October of 1981, she was a pioneer in the formation of the National Garifuna Council.

Auntie Madé, as we affectionately call her, is a mother, grandmother, wife, farmer, poet, actress, and choreographer. Since 1972, she has been actively engaged in the preparation and training of candidates for the Miss Garifuna Belize National Contest. Under her excellent training, many beautiful young ladies from Hopkins Village have won that contest.

All her life Auntie Madé has been writing poems and prayers and recording them in her book in Garifuna and in English. In all her writing she insists that it be written in both languages. As a practising linguist, she is also concerned about the standardization of Garifuna orthography.

For her contribution to the promotion, preservation and retrieval of Garifuna culture, tradition, music and dances, Mrs. Marcella Lewis was recently awarded a Citation by the National Garifuna Council. A few of her poems were published in 1977 in a Garifuna anthology entitled Chülüha Dan (It's About Time).

Auntie Madé has travelled and visited several countries including Guatemala, Honduras, Saint Vincent, United States of America, and Canada. She is a cultural ambassador for Belize, promoting her culture wherever she goes. She is indeed a Belizean patriot. A few years ago, Mrs. Lewis was honoured by the United Garifuna Association of New York.

For the past two years, Auntie Madé has given much of her time to the production of the People's Garifuna Dictionary.

Mrs. Marcella Lewis is a commisioned Lay Minister and actively involved in the evangelization of Hopkins. She is a very spiritual person and this spirituality manifests itself in great inspiring poems like *Béibuga Luma Inarüni* (Walk With Truth).

Sebastian Cayetano and Fabian Cayetano

Garinagu Sarawama: Chülüha Dan

Garinagu sarawama,
Chülüha dan.
Ñübiwama lidoun aban.
Hurawamei fanidira,
Iñurawaméi wamalali,
Keimoun wabaronguoun.

Garinagu, mágurawaméi wanasiun;
Adimurehawaméi wereru;
Pantawamá lau wereru, niduheñu;
Gamalaliwamá aganbúa wamamuga,
Dará lámuga bena wabá
    lun webelurun luei huya.
Buchá wawagu ahuyúa.
Wasanigu Garinagu, eyeriun, hianriun-
Dügüwama, wídeha luagu lawanseru
    wageira
Haranseha wayunagu wabá.
Lun súdara badíüla háratiun,
Lúyawa, lemenigirame wageira
    le Balisi,
Wabien, libime wabien.

Garinagu Arise: The Time Has Come

Garifuna arise,
The time has come.
Be as one.
Wave our flag,
Raise our voice,
Let us go forward!

Garinagu, let us not abandon our roots;
Let us speak our language;
Let us be proud of our language, kinfolks;
Let us have a voice so we may be heard,
So the door may be open for us to come in
    from the rain.
We are tired of being in the rain.
Our Garifuna children, boys and girls,
Let us stand and help in the advancement
    of our homeland
Established for us by our ancestors.
You must be brave soldiers,
Guardians, and support our homeland
    Belize,
Our home, sweet home.

Nageira

Balisi, bisien nun an!
Nageira, lau sun biñüraü le,
Baganóu nun kei furumieguárügü
    Úburugu wéiriti.

Pántatina bau.
Garinagu agübürigu, isanigu,
Gada lubadiwa libagari Balisi

Wídeha lidoun lawanseru wageira;
Mama lau dimurei, lau adügaü.

Hurawamei lufanidira wageira
    Balisi lau ugundani.
Wiñureime wamalali lidoun aban igabüri
Maguraba wamá haruga;
    Uguñele.
Husewama gasu,
Wabaruaguon wamá lau wadasi,
Ítara wamá kei ágila lau erei
Buiti lun wageira, Balisi,
    Kátaya yádiwa la.
Wabien, libime wabien.

Ánhawa añura agurabaha
Leíbagubádiwa dan;
Wágawaha ba serenu;
Wágawaha ligía me serenu
    kábagi asusereda?

My Home

Belize, how much I love you!
My home, though you are small,
To me you are like the biggest city
  In the world.

I am proud of you.
Garinagu, old and young,
We enjoy the life of Belize.

We help to improve our home;
Not with words, with deeds.

Wave the flag of our home,
  Belize, with gladness,
Raise our voice with one accord.
Do not wait for tomorrow;
  Start today.
Be brave,
Go forward with our work,
Be like the eagle so strong
Good to our home, Belize,
  Regardless of who you are.
Our home, sweet home.

If we sit and wait,
  Time will run us over;
We will be wet by dew;
What will happen
  If we would be wet by dew?

Nuragate

Nagurúa kei Marcella Flores, lisani Telesfores Flores tau Simona Augustine Flores, disi sisi lidan Eneru, lidan irumu milu nefu san wein. Biámañanu nibirian: aban disi irumu luweya nuei, le aban seingü irumu. Aban irumu nau tonwe wáguchu. Lubabei naweyadu lun nidin leskuela túmañadina liduhe núguchi, Louisa Martinez. Tábouguña Riversdale houn harutian lúbien aban Ingleisi. Tiúbudiri agounigirubalina.

Sisi irumu nau aba nidin lun Seinbeidi lun nidin leskuela. Aba túmañadina la nagütü, lóufuri núguchi, Cornelia Flores Martinez. Biama irumu lau núguchi tonwe lúguchu aba tanügüni lagütü. Dan le tonwe lagütü, gádürü irumu lau. Aba tanügüni lóufuri. Disi sisi irumu lau lígiru Dangrigagien. Ladüga tamarieidún lóufuri luma Secundo Matinez, aban Seinbeidina, aba heidi Seinbeidin.

Lidan falumágei leredera náruguti, Marcelino Augustine, túguchi núguchu, lubadu Seinbeidi. Añaheingua linebafani ñei. Úagiru meha leskuela Seinbeidi. Aba teredera núguchu Dangriga luma tiáwürite, Francisco Augustine.

Hísientina houn niduhenu. Haríenga nun,
"Durati bau, Chuti bau."
"Walagan" lian háwaru nun ladüga tonwe núguchu.

Furumien uremu nadüga widü irumu nau. Aba nidin anüga duna tuma niduhe. Dan wachülürü liumoun duna, aba tariengu, "Anihein aban mafia ya." Aba wéibagu. Aba neremuha:

One day Tiofila gone by the well.
Suddenly Alba called,
"Nihán aban mafia!"
Tiofila run, wawaguéina.

Aban weyu wéidian árabu anüga awasi, baruru, gániesi, saragu katei lun wéigi. Wuribati larihi dan luagu binafi ligía. Aba labachougadu. Aba narihi dúeirugu, bachouga. Aba neremuha:

6

My Story

I was born Marcella Flores, daughter of Telefores Flores and Simona Augustine Flores, in Dangriga on January 16, 1920. I had two brothers, one 10 years older and one five years older. My mother died when I was one year old. Before I was old enough to go to school, I was with my father's cousin, Louisa Martinez, who was a cook at Riversdale, the home of an English family. While she cooked, the white lady minded me.

When I was 6 years old, I moved to Seine Bight to go to school. I lived with my father's aunt, Cornelia Flores Martinez. His mother had died when he was two years old, so he went to live with his grandmother, but she died when he was four, so his aunt raised him. They lived in Dangriga until he was 16 years old when they moved to Seine Bight because his aunt married Secundo Martinez who lived there.

My mother's father, Marcelino Augustine, had a coconut plantation near Seine Bight. His descendents still live there. But Seine Bight had no school in those days, so my mother lived in Dangriga with her father's brother, Francisco Augustine, to go to school.

My mother's relatives loved me. They said,

"You are so smart. You have great understanding."

They called me, "Walagan" which means our legacy, the legacy of my mother who had died.

I composed my first song when I was 8 years old. I went to get water with my cousin. When we reached the mouth of the river, she called, a ghost is here!" So, we all ran. While we were running, I sang:

> One day Tiofila gone by the well.
> Suddenly Alba called,
> "There's a ghost here!"
> Tiofila ran, shouting as she went.

One day we were going to the plantation to get corn, plantain, cane, so many good things to eat. At first the weather was no good. Then the weather came out very pretty. So I sang:

Buiti binafi, lubuidu larugan wau
Wariha lun weyu,
Durungua, ma larugounga;
Durungua, ma laruma lau.
Le libime láfuaru
Darí lun ibidie la nun
Kábala nerere.

Danme nariwachagu,
Wáhuma houn numadagu
   hama nubesinanigu.
Danme nariwachagu
Haríenga me tun numada
"Ñüda bumada, téibuga águyu,
Téibuga emeragua, téibuga águyu
   Téibuga emeragua, téibuga águyu." (music p. 52)

Aba lagaindu nati nun.
"Meremuhaba ya! Hísienti uremu bun! Wéiriha biúmagu!"
Luéigienrügü uremu aba leíbahanina. Aba neíbagu tiúnagien guríara lun tígirin.

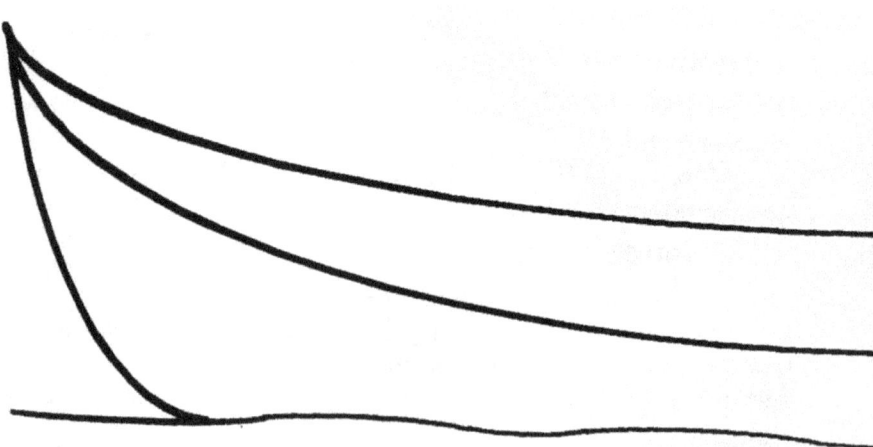

Beautiful morning,
Beautiful morning
Look at the sun so bright;
Look at the sun so bright;
It looks so sweet
I do not know
What to say.

When I am dying,
Call my friends
    and neighbors.
When I am dying,
Tell my best friend
"Your friend is going home,
Your friend is going to her rest,
Your friend is going home."

My brother was annoyed with me.
"Don't sing! You like to sing! You have such a big mouth!"
Then, for the sake of a song, he chased me. I ran from the stern to the bow of the dory.

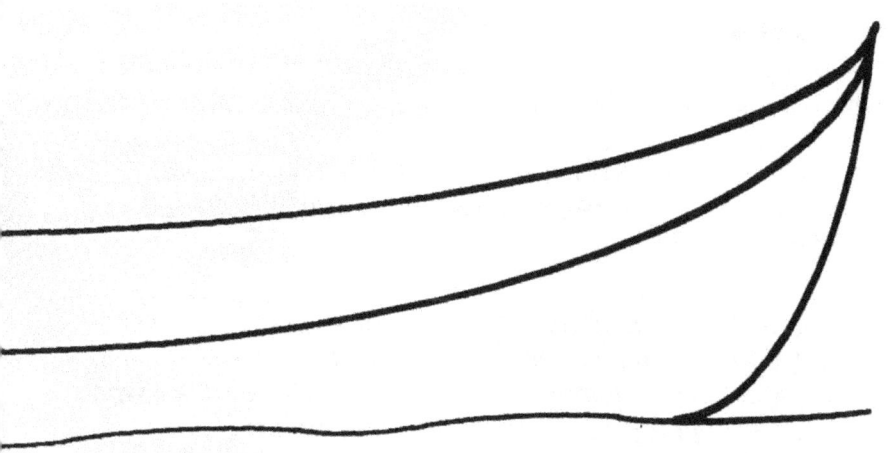

Lúmagien disi irumu nau darí lumoun uguñe le, neremuhaña ligilisirugu.
Mabuchahatína meha leskuela. Nadaguba uremu, soprano, alto, tenor, bass hau nánigu. Aba wareinchu. Aba lagabuni adundeihati,
"Katei lira? Badügatia Marcella!"
Aba nanügü busiganu.
"Aganba nei."
Aba weidi lun. Aba weremuhani lun. Aba láhayachun.

Sagü irumu wáhureru lubá tadouragu leskuela. Añarei wádagien mabürüdadi, malihadi. Aba nadundeihanian. Dan liabi wáhurerun, buíti. Úati mégeiti; lidan dan. Laríenga adundeihati,
"Marcella, ídaliansa badügüni? Sian nubalin lau sun nadundeihañala."
Sügünumutu tisisi lau katorusu irumu. Rédeitina leskuela dagá lumoun disi sisi irumu. Aba nerederu meme aturiaha, ídeha leskuelarugu, akurakahoun hawadigimari, adundeiha lubá wan huraraü.

Aba lálügüdünina nidin luma Dangriga lun naseiniru lun narufudaha. Úagiru meha kolohiu; ñüdütina hamuga. Máhatina lun nidin. Magurasutina habá irahüñü. Ladüga mabuchahatian. Sákürinali. Uguñe le anahagua ídeha leskuela.

Disi sedu irumu nau aba nadaraduha luma Victor Lewis. Aba nidin luma Seinbeidigien lun Ñontón. Lidoun irumu milu nefu san bian wein, anihein aban liáwan dan. Aba labuinchuni duna fulasu. Aba wádinu lun yahoun Yugadoun. Yahaña sedü familia wabá. Honduragien hayabi lidan irumu 1937 aluaha múñasu yahoun Balisi.

Lidoun irumu milu nefu san darandi sedü tagurúa nisani Julia. Lidoun irumu milu nefu san darandi nefu lagurúa nisani eyeri furumienti, Solomon. Lidoun irumu milu nefu san bian wein aban lagurúa nisani eyeri habíama, Francis. Wein sisi ñanu nibaña, wein yanu nílawagu.

From the age of ten years old, up to now, I sang in the choir at church.

I used to be mischievious in school. I would make up songs, soprano, alto, tenor, and bass, with my fellow students. We made a lot of noise. The teacher said,

"What is all this noise? It must be you, Marcella."

I felt ashamed.

"Let me hear it."

We went up to his desk and sang for him and then he smiled.

We trained to put on an entertainment at the end of each school year. Some of the children could not read and write, so I trained them for their parts in the play. When the play took place, no mistakes happened. The teacher said,

"Marcella, how did you do this? How do you train them? I cannot do it and I am the teacher."

I passed Standard 6 when I was 14 years old, but in those days, we stayed in school until we were 16, so the teacher didn't want me to leave. So I stayed and took higher studies with the teacher. I helped in the school, correcting the students' work and training them for entertainments.

My teacher took me to Dangriga to sign up to teach. In those days there was no college or I would have gone. But I refused. I had no patience with the children. Some were sassy. Now I am sorry. Up till now I still help in the school.

When I was 17, I fell in love with Victor Lewis. We left Seine Bight and moved to New Town. In 1941 there was a hurricane and New Town became even lower with all the waves washing in, so the whole town moved to Hopkins. There were already seven families living there who had come from Honduras in 1937 when people were being killed there. They came to Belize for freedom.

My daughter, Julia, was born in 1937; my eldest son, Solomon, was born in 1939, and my second son, Francis, was born in 1941. I have 26 living grandchildren and 20 living great-grandchildren.

Adügadina saragu weyasu. Lidan irumu milu nefu san gádürü wein biama nagumesera adundeihaña lurúeiti wefedu wagía Garinagu. Ligía furumien lagañeiru Hopkins. Ábaya wagañeiru bian irumu lárigien. Adügatiwa wéyasu Niu Yakü luagu wagañeiru. Aba háwaru lun wábuti, Felix Miranda,

"Ka uégie miabi habéi lun Chicago. Busiéntiwa gien warihinian."

Lidoun irumu milu nefu san gádürü wein disi adügatina weyasu lun Yurumein hageira wayunagu. Aba wábürügü Barbados tuéigien lugunena dúreiru kéibüri ladaünrü gádürü rabounwéyu. Aba warumagu ñei. Laruga binafi tiabi Sister Nel anügawa hamoun Garinagu. Dísegien wagía hirimichahadíwa tagüle faluma. Narienga houn nánigu,

"Madisedügiadiwa. Hirimichadina hagüledina Garinagu."

Wachülürü, sun katei areinseli wabá. Aba híchuguni gágamuru nun, narienga houn,

"Gúndaguadina, hirimichana wagüledina. Subudi nali hageira ñadiwa la Garínagu."

Aba héheraha.

Aba hanügüniwa luagu ubouhu Balliceaux ñei lubéi hadaürúa wayunagu. Nuguya agumuhoúni areira. Lichugúa gágamuru luágu niuma, aba nadimureha. Nadeiragua nungua bulé náguira. Adadagaradina. Sian nadimureha. Aba lariengu Paul, le ñüdübei wau,

"Susereti le houn sun huguya ha átürü baña ya. Subuditi ka la uéigien?"

"Ka uéigien?"

"Ladüga hata hiúnagu le áwiuhabei ya."

I have made many journeys. From 1982 I started to train the young women who competed for Queen of Garifuna Settlement Day. That was the first year Hopkins won. Two years later we won again and the winner was awarded a trip to New York. I went along as her trainer. From Chicago, they called our host, Felix Miranda, and said,

"Why don't they also come to Chicago? We must see them here."

In 1990 I went to Saint Vincent, the home of our ancestors. The plane landed in Barbados at four o'clock in the afternoon, so we slept there. The next morning Sister Nel took us to Gregs, where the Garinagu live. From far away we could smell coconut oil. I said to my companions,

"We must be near. I smell the oil of Garinagu."

When we reached, everything was ready for us. They put a microphone to my mouth and I said,

"I enjoyed my trip because, as I reached here, I could smell coconut oil. I know I am in the land of Garinagu."

They all laughed.

They took us to Balliceaux, the island where our ancestors were held captive. When we landed, I was the last one to get out of the dory. They put the microphone to my mouth to speak about my landing. I started to talk. All of a sudden I choked. The tears flowed. I trembled. Paul, our host, said,

"That happens to every one of you who lands here. You know why?"

"Why?"

"The blood of your ancestors flowed here."

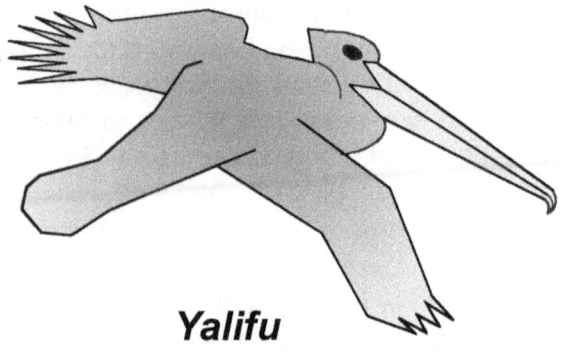

Yalifu

Yalifu, wíreiguáñaha buguya dúeirugu,
Mama lubuídu bidani.
Gimugatina bun
Ítara nuguya hamuga keisi buguya.

Yalifu, aüdü le ñei lumuti babusuera
Bachülürü,
Chülütibu.
Mabusuerútibu paséi.

Rubei bufuruma nun ítara námuga
Kei buguya.
Aban arünei buiti buguya
Baranaha keisi dúeirugu.

Ruba paséi nun.
Barübana lábugien barüna
Báguraname lubeya Yurumein
Le hageira wayunagu,
Lageira Satuye lau
    Ilehu Binéin.
Seremein nuba bun.

Pelican

Pelican, you keep soaring in the sky,
You have such a good time.
How I envy you
I wish I were like you.

Pelican, whatever place
You want to reach,
You will reach.
You don't need passage.

Give me your shape so I may
Be like you.
You are a good captain
At sea and in the sky.

Give me passage.
Take me under your wings
Throw me on the shores of Saint Vincent
The home of our ancestors,
The home of Chatoyer and
    Alejo Beni.
I will be grateful to you.

Lubuidu Láfuaru Hati

Lubuidu láfuaru hati
Úara luma lañuragu weyu,
Ehesebedágüdaña gürigia.

Hati, gumadi bumuti ubóu
    Hau sun lílagu.
Dagá hamoun waruguma bagumadiru.
Chülüti aban weyu báfuaru
    Hau ürüwa waruguma:
        Aban luéigien bónwere,
        Aban luéigien bubaüna,
        Aban bárigi.
Kati uádigimari lira?
Anirein dan hagía bubá,
    Buguya hárigi.
Halía sa hébeda?

Hati, hália ñadibu sa
    Luagu ürüwa weyu
        Bálüdagu lubaya bagiribudu?
Súntina asaminara ída lian la.
    Áluaha numuti,
        Madari numuti.
Bígirawa lidan luburiga.

How Beautiful the Moonrise

How beautiful the moonrise
Just as the sun eases down,
Filling all with a feeling of contentment.

Moon, you rule the earth
    With all it contains.
Even the stars are subject to you.
A certain day comes and you appear
    With three stars:
        One on your right,
        One on your left,
        And one following you.
Whose work is that?
At times, they are in front,
    And you behind them.
Where do you all end up?

Moon, where are you
    For those three days
        You disappear before you return?
I wonder how it is.
    I've sought the answer everywhere,
        I have not found it.
You leave us in the dark.

Lubuidu Láfuaru Weyu Binafi

Lubuidu láfuaru weyu binafi
Íchiga arugoungani lun ubóu.
Chahinha lari barana le lugunda;
Óurabahówa tubana wewe le lugunda;
Laríenhe abürühati lau
   Ladimurehañala.
Kasa lererubei? Ka lererubei?

Wariha luagu wübü,
Ma tiluma wewe
   Hau sun hawíeri dunuru,
     Ámuñeguéinarügü hayu;
   Hau sun hawíeri íliru
     Ámuñeguéinarügü hagabüri
        Lun wawiwandu hawagu.
Kati adüga lira?

Wagararagúa wariha baranahoun,
   Añahan sun hawíeri üdüraü
        Lun wabagaridu hawagu.
Kasa adüga lira?
Niduheñu, ka san adüga lira?

Irumurugu
   Hilá fuluri,
     Chagala lílewei.
Láhuyu huya,
   Hilumagua,
     Ma libime líheme.
Kati adüga lira?

How Beautiful the Sunrise

How beautiful the sunrise
Giving light to the earth.
The sea grins, happily showing its teeth;
The leaves on the trees happily frolic ;
The writer says
    They are all speaking.
What do they say? What do they say?

We look at the mountains.
Such healthy trees
    With all kinds of birds,
        With different types of feathers;
    With all kinds of game animals
        Each with its own manner
            For us to live on.
Who made all this?

We turn around, and look to the sea,
    Here are all types of fish
        For us to live on
Who made all this?
My people, who made all this?

In the dry season.
    Flowers die,
        And drop their blossoms.
When it rains,
    Flowers bloom again.
        How sweet it smells.
Who made all this?

Irumurugu wáchuga wachari,
Wábuna baruru,
Wábuna yami,
Wábuna wahü,
Wábuna guchu,
Wábuna mabi.
    Lemeñagua irumu:
        Dibirüga baruru,
        Bougua mua tau yami,
        Bougua mua tau wahü,
        Bougua mua tau guchu,
        Bougua mua tau mabi.
    Kati adüga lira?
Kasa adüga lira?
Le wáwarubei Wabureme Súntigabáfu.

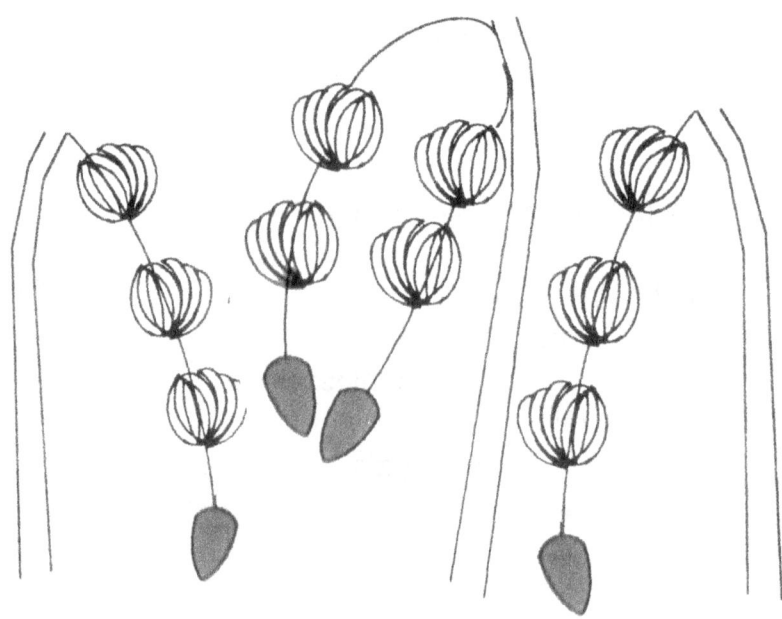

In the dry season, we cut our plantation,
We plant plantains,
We plant yams,
We plant coco,
We plant yampa,
We plant potatoes.
    When the year is replaced:
        Plantains hang everwhere,
        The earth bursts with yams,
        The earth bursts with coco,
        The earth bursts with yampa,
        The earth bursts with potatoes,
        And what is the cause of all this?
Who made all this?
He whom we call our Maker, the Almighty.

Wéyasu

Luagu aban weyu nadüga wéyasu
    Péinigien lun Córozali
Nágurei nagu
    Luagu bian louba üma
Anunhán sun túyeri ídibu
    Aruruha lóubawagu üma
        Bürü barihin
            Kamá le bunawaguárügütu.
Sun ídibu to
    Luntu taseriwiduníwa.
Banügei béyabugien anunha ya
    Túyerigu ídibu
        Laru laru beya
Sun ídibu to
    Lúntugien taseriwiduníwa
Kátei san gabafubei, wéiribei ubafu,
    Ábunagubaru ídibu to ítara ibe?
Marihíniwa lubéi luagu rügü
    Hamuga aban weyu ábunagua?
Kátei funa san ábunaguti le Marihínbei?
Subuditi san hun nuéi?
Káteisa gabafuti le?
Niduheñu!
    Másura wamá asaminara.
Máma dügü funasa
    Wabureme Súntigabáfu?
Samina huméi san numa.

Journey

One day I made a journey
    From Punta Gorda to Corozal.
I looked around
    From one side of the road to the other
All kinds of trees
    Right by the side of the road
        As far as you can see
            As if they were planted.
All these trees
    Are good for us to use.
And turn toward the sea
    All kinds of trees
        Along the beach.
All these trees
    Are good for us to use.
Who has the power
    To plant so many trees?
There is not a day
    When planting was seen
Who plants that is not seen?
Do you know so you may tell me?
Who is this powerful?
My people
    Let us not wonder.
Was it not
    Our Master, the Almighty?
Think with me.

Béibuga Luma Inarüni

Béibuga luma inarüni.
Ladundeirubadibu inarüni lidoun üma le richabei.
Bachugeraguba luagu béibugu;
Máhüchüraba.
Waba luagu Wabureme;
Líchugubei lúhobu bun
Ladüga anirein buma.

Bubaronguóun, béibuga luma inarüni.
Ladundeirubádibu inarüni lidoun üma le richabei.

Láhuyubadibu huya,
Sü lábume weyu.
Makeraba.
Babeluruba lidoun luburiga;
Waba tuagu Lúguchu Wabureme.
Táfuaruba waruguma to durungua timá boun;
Tadundeirubadibu lidoun larugounga.

Bubaronguóun, béibuga luma inarüni.
Ladundeirubádibu inarüni lidoun üma le richabei.

Ñéibei weyu bayahuagu bówagua
Gumuha bugurasu
Waba luagu Súntigabáfu
Líderubádibu, bachülürüba lau aban ugundani
Anhein afíen bubéi lidan Wabureme

Bubaronguóun, béibuga luma inarüni
Ladundeirubádibu inarüni lidoun üma le richabei.

Lidan liri Úguchili,
Lidan liri Irahü,
Lidan liri Áfurugu Gúnfuliti.
Ítara la

Walk with Truth

Walk with Truth.
Truth will lead you on the right way.
You might stumble on your way;
Do not be afraid.
Call on the Master;
He will stretch out his hands to you.
For he is with you.

Walk with Truth.
Truth will lead you in the right way.

It will rain on you,
The sun will burn you.
Do not complain.
You will enter into darkness;
Call on the Mother of our Savior.
The brightest star will appear;
She will lead you to Light.

Walk with Truth.
Truth will lead you in the right way.

There will be days when you cry,
Your patience gone.
Call on the Almighty;
He will help you; you will arrive with gladness
If you believe in our Master.

Walk with Truth.
Truth will lead you in the right way.

In the name of the Father,
In the name of the Son,
In the name of the Holy Spirit.
Amen

Hísienti Nageira Nun

Hísienti nageira nun.
Ma nísebe sawanarugu,
Fufu garabali
Wáwalu libían Súntigabáfu.

Hísientima bei nun
Dan wásügürü tuagu lugunena múa.
Ma lubuidu larumugu lídibu gudi,
Sian warihini wübü;
Darugua lau gúmulali.

Aba nareiru lun néñeguhani
Nachülürü luagu wübü ni murusu watu ñei
Kása uéigien lagumulahábei, niduheñu,
Ligía úati watu luagu?
Aba nagiribudu, neredera lau saminaü

Hísienti Sawana Nun (Uremu)

Hísienti sawana nun;
Hísienti duna churunruti
 le ñei bei nun;
Hísienti fuluri
 le ñei bei nun;
Hísienti hagúaraha gurewegi
 ha ñei baña nun,
  tuéigien tídibu wewe.

Hísienti lahunha duna churunruti
 le ñei bei nun;
Hísienti lahunha garabali
 le ñei bei nun;
Hísienti hagúaraha gurewegi
 ha ñei baña nun,
  tuéigien tídibu wewe.   (music p. 56)

I Love My Home

I love my home.
How I love the savannah,
I enjoy the sea breeze
With the sounds of the creatures of the Almighty.

What I love the most
While we are passing in a bus.
Is how beautiful the leaping of the pine trees,
We cannot see the mountains;
They are covered in smoke.

I get out to put out the fire.
When I get to the mountain, there is no fire.
Why is there smoke, my people,
And there is no fire?
I turn back in wonder.

I Love the Savannah (Song)

I love the savannah;
I love its fresh water;

I love its flowers;

I love the calls
of the parrots
from the trees.

I love the sound of its river;
I love the sound
of the wind out there;

I love the calls
of the parrots
from the trees.

Duna Churunruti Dangriga

Duna churunruti Dangriga,
Niabian lun nadügüni nuwéyasun.
   Dan narihi añahan sun hawíeri dunúru
     Dagouga luagu sandube
        Liúmoun duna.

Aba náhudurunί niágumari
   Óunigiraña dunuru ha lau aban saminaü:
Ída lian la haganbagu houngua lidan lubéi aban
Hínchei hagibu.

Lau méme ñadina saminaü le;
Dan narihi hamagua dunuru ha.
Aban meme ñei lumuti háhamachagúa;
   Núrurugun.

Narienga núnguarügü:
"Ka funa san hóuchubei dunuru ha harufudaha nun?"
Noúnabagua nungua,
"Harufudahaña
   Ísien, inebeguaü úniguaü,
   Aganbaguni,
   Íderagua woungua.
Wayabi me lidoun aban
Keisi aban rasa
Kei dunuru ha."
   Ligíaba wawanseru.

Stann Creek River

Stann Creek River,
I was going to make a voyage.
    When I saw all kinds of birds
        On the sandbar
                At the mouth of the river.

While I pushed the pole, I turned
    And watched the birds with wonder:
How they hear each other
How they all face one direction

I was still wondering
When I saw all these birds.
Fly away in the same direction;
    To the North.

I said to myself:
"What are these birds trying to teach me?"
I answer myself,
"They are teaching
    Love, respect for one another ,
    Concern for one another,
    Cooperation;
Then we will come together as one
As one race
Like these birds."
    This is the way we will advance.

Kalifónia

Luagu aban weyu,
Neíbuga laru beya Meriga
   Lun nágawaha barana.
Díseginian nihán aban sánsiguaü
   Baranaha.
Nararama naríagua.
Níhan aban gáluma,
   Miriha barana
      Dagá lumoun leben barihi.

Ariha nuguya
   Núrurugún,
   Suedirugún,
   Nawestarugún,
   Sawestarugún,
   Dúreirugún.
Mirigua dúeirugu,
Nin murusun dáseiti,
Nin dunuru máhamahatian.

Siángili nagoun
   Ariagua.
Aba nadunrún.
      " Katei san?"
Lian umalali,
   "Bágawa".
Nagararagúa, bian gürigia
   Ibidietian nun.

California

One day,
I went to the seaside in the States
    To bathe in the sea.
From afar I saw a change
    In the sea.
I stood and watched,
There was a great calm,
    The sea shone
        As far as the eye could see.

I looked
    To the north,
    To the south,
    To the northwest,
    To the southwest,
    To the sky.
The sky shone,
Not a stain in the heavens,
Not even birds flew.

I could not bathe
    For watching.
Then I was touched.
        "What is it?"
A voice from behind,
    "Bathe".
I turned around and saw two people
    I did not know.

Aba nanufudedagun
 "Manufudedagua ba.
  Bágawa".

Hadabura nubá,
 Nuguya hárigi.
Sandinei laburuchagunina
 Barana le lidili.
Wáfuliha suédirugún,
Nadeirarugua nungua
Seingü guadiwa:
 Bian nubá,
 Bian nárigi.

Ma larugounga barana;
Saragu narihi baranaha
 Marihinágili lúmagien nibagari.
Hanufudegua buguya hamuga,
Añahan nugurasu, núniri,
 Úara numa.
Kátaña la,
Inhin!

(Lidan irumu 1989 barühamutina nibaña Kalifónia. Busíentifuna Kalifónia laganbagu luóugua aba líchugunina lidoun uénedi.)

I was frightened
   "Do not be afraid.
     Bathe"

They jumped into the sea before me,
   I followed them.
I felt the pressure
   of the cold water.
We swam to the southwest.
Then I realized
There were five of us:
   Two ahead of me,
   Two behind me.

How clear was the sea;
I saw much in the sea
   That I had never seen in my life.
You would have been afraid,
But here, giving me courage,
   were my guardians, along with me
Who were they?
I do not know!

(In 1989 I went to visit my grandchildren in California. California must have wanted a poem about itself so it gave me a dream.)

Áfaraha Ta Garadun Mesu

Luagu aban dan tadaraduha garadun luma mesu. Tau asaminara kabalá tadüga anhein ñei mégeiti haganagua ladüga hianru to hanufudetu luei eyeri le.

Wéiriou luma wéiriei,
"Ki ki ki ki,"
Hínchuahaña wéinamuhaña ha.

Luagu dügü lubéi aban weyu lídangien sun weyu, layanuha tun, móunabutu. Ladimureha tun, móunabutu. Tuóugua ñoú funa. Méigitian funa tun.

Leíbahoun, téibagua luei.
Aba tasaminarun kabalá tadüga lun táfarahani tuáriyua. Tachubara luagu lidan magaradahan la.

Tágürei larigei, lígiri, liumaru.
"Miau, miau, aürü, aürü."
Láwaragua lun tárügüdün luei.

Niduheñu, sánsigua sígulu; áfaraha ta garadun mesu!

The Mouse Beat the Cat!

There was a time, when a mouse had an affair with a cat. The mouse wondered what she would do if anything would happen because she was afraid of this fellow.

We could hear them laughing,
"Ki ki ki ki,"
They are romancing each other.

One day of all days the cat wanted to converse with the mouse, but she did not respond. He spoke to her, but she did not answer. She must have been in a bad mood. She did not want to play.

He chased her and she ran from him.

She considered what she would do to beat him, so he would not overcome her. She turned and jumped on him, surprising him.

She bit his ears, his nose, his lips.

"Meow, meow, awroo, awroo!"

He screamed so someone would pull her away from him.

My people, times have changed. The mouse beat the cat!

(Victor Lewis, my husband, went to South Stann Creek one day and saw a mouse playing with a cat. He was surprised and commented to the man who lived there. "They do it all the time," he said. Victor told this to me and I wrote this story.)

Uguñe Haweyuri Sun Úguchuru

Buiti guñou houn sun úguchuru. Furumienti katei, rúwama seremein lun Wabureme, Súntigabáfu, hawagu úguchuru hau wasanigu, ha lafuredeirubaña woun, luma luagu sun katei.

Uguñe haweyuri sun úguchuru. Gíbeti wadasi houn wasanigu. Higougu úguchurugunigu, lárama wamá keisi agübürigu, ebu derebugutian.

Lúmagien lañurun irahü gawarahali tagúmeseru úguchuru adundeiha. Lúmagien lanumeihóuniwa lasuseihóuña óunigirei látuadi o tátuadi luei sandi.

Eibu haweinamudu aweirideina gien wadasi lun hadundeirúniwa lidoun le buídubei, le lunbei seríwibei la houn, lacherúniwa houn luei lagübüri.

Haritaguatina le tímati wadasi, wagía úguchurunígu, wáfagun lun wíchugu furendei houn; wóunahanian leskuela. Gíbeti lúyeri furendei lun hafurendeiruni isanigu lun habagaridun luagu. Anhein hísienhabéi wasanigu woun, wáfagua hawagu.

Isanigu, aganbúa ta úguchuru. Inebewa ta úguchuru. Hísienwa ta úguchuru; áfagatá sun lúyeri. Ka lá hamabuchahan isanigu, hísiengían tun úguchuru. Máhatiwa hau.

Seremein nian hun.

Today We Honor All Mothers

Good night to all mothers. First, let us give thanks to our Savior, the Almighty, for mothers and our children, whom He has lent to us, and for everything else.

Today we honor all mothers. We have many tasks to do for our children. Come, mothers, let us stand as a firm foundation.

From the time the baby starts to sit, a mother could start to train the child. From the time the child is born, you keep them clean and protect the boy or girl from sickness.

The more they grow, the more work we have to do to lead them to things which will be good for them and away from those which are bad.

I think the best thing, we mothers can do, is to try to give our children education; to send them to school. There are many kinds of knowledge they need to learn to live in this world. If we love our children, we will do our best for them.

Children, listen to your mother. Respect your mother. Love your mother. She suffers all kinds of things. Even when children misbehave, the mother loves them. She does not want them to get hurt.

Thank you.

Lubuidu Namule Eyeri

Lubuidu namule eyeri.
Sisi hati lau uguñe.
Lau sun maríengadi la
Aganba lumuti nereru lun.
Dan le nayarafadu lurugabun
Aba lóurabahóuniwa.
Wéiriti lisien nun;
Namule raü eyeri eyeri,
Wéiriti lisien nun.
Namule raü eyeri, eyeri.   (music p. 66)

My Pretty Baby Brother

My pretty baby brother.
He is six months old today.
Though he cannot speak
He hears whatever I say.
When I get near to him
He jumps with joy.
Oh, how I love him;
My brother, my boy,
Oh, how I love him.
My brother, my boy.

(This was a reading in my school book. I translated it into Garifuna and made a lullaby to sing to my baby brother.)

Keimoun Numa

Keimoun numa, numadagunu,
 áluahei Chécheche.
Keimoun numa, numadagunu,
 áluahei Chécheche.
Keimoun numa, numadagunu,
 áluahei; lüya - Eh!
Keimoun numa lárigi Che
 áluahei, numadagunu;
Keimoun numa, keimoun numa, keimoun numa

Tigemeri wádigidigi
 ligemeribei árabu.
Tigemeri wádigidigi
 ligemeribei árabu.
Tarugounga wádigidigi
 ligemeribei árabu.
Keimoun numa lárigi Che,
 áluahei, numadagunu;
Keimoun numa, keimoun numa, keimoun numa

Tálüdagu wádigidigi,
 lagúarahan Chécheche.
Tálüdagu wádigidigi,
 lagúarahan Chécheche.
Tálüdagu wádigidigi,
 lagúarahan árabu.
Keimoun numa lárigi Che,
 áluahei, numadagunu,
Keimoun numa, keimoun numa, keimoun numa

(music p. 56)

Come With Me

Come with me, my friends,
    and look for Checheche.
Come with me, my friends,
    and look for Checheche.
Come with me, my friends,
    and look; for he is lost - Uh!
Come with me, follow Che,
    look for him, my friends
Come with me, come with me, come with me

The light of the firefly
    is his light in the bush.
The light of the firefly
    is his light in the bush.
The flash of the firefly
    is his light in the bush.
Come with me, follow Che,
    look for him, my friends;
Come with me, come with me, come with me

When the firefly disappears,
    he will cry, Checheche.
When the firefly disappears,
    he will cry, Checheche.
When the firefly disappears,
    he will cry in the bush.
Come with me, follow Che,
    look for him, my friends
Come with me, come with me, come with me

(This song is from one of the plays which I have written and produced. The little boy, Checheche, is lost and the whole community goes out into the bush to find him.)

Mábuiga María

Mábuiga María,
　　Buíntibu lau gürasia, furíegi ba wau.
Mábuiga María,
　　Buíntibu lau gürasia, furíegi ba wau.
Wáguchu Gúnfulitu, ruba erei wau.
Wáguchu Gúnfulitu, ruba erei wau.
Úguchuru lurúeite sielu, furíegi ba wau.
Úguchuru lurúeite sielu, furíegi ba wau.
Badimureha wawagu lun Wabureme.
Bayumuragua wau lun Wabureme.

(music p. 58)

Lúguchu Wabureme

Lúguchu Wabureme,
Lúguchu Súntigabáfu,
Nihán lianwan dan; wátiwa buagu.
Nihán lianwan dan; wátiwa buagu.

Lúguchu Wasalubaraha,
Lúguchu Wabungiute,
Wáguchu, bámaliha wau;
Wáguchu, bámaliha wau.

Higabu woun, Wáguchi.
Higabu woun, Súntigabáfu.
Gudeme wamá bun, ferudun bawa;
Gudeme wamá bun, ferudun bawa.

(music p. 59)

Hail Mary

Hail Mary,
  Full of Grace, pray for us.
Hail Mary,
  Full of Grace, pray for us.
Holy Mother, give us strength.
Holy Mother, give us strength.
Mother, Queen of Heaven, pray for us.
Mother, Queen of Heaven, pray for us.
Speak for us to our Master.
Intercede for us to our Master.

(This and the other hymns in this book have come to me complete with the music, usually when I wake up.)

Mother of Our Savior

Mother of Our Savior,
Mother of the Almighty,
There is a hurricane; we call on you.
There is a hurricane; we call on you.

Mother of Our Savior,
Mother of Our God,
Our Mother, intercede for us;
Our Mother, intercede for us.

Come to us, Our Father.
Come to us, Almighty.
Have mercy on us, forgive us;
Have mercy on us, forgive us.

(This hymn was composed during a hurricane in Dangriga.)

Wáguchu Gúnfulitu

Wáguchu gúnfulitu,
  Arufudabei bémeri woun.
Lúguchu Wabureme,
  Buíngüdabei bisien woun.
Lúguchu Wabungiute,
  Bihatiri le, inebewalá.

Gudeme wamá bun, Guadalupe,
  Birahüñü gusa wagía, wísien bun.
Gudeme wamá bun, Labirihein,
  Birahüñü gusa wagía, bísien woun.
Gudeme wamá bun, Wáguchu,
  Birahüñü gusa wagía, Wáguchu.

(music p. 60)

Úguchuru, Arufudabawa

Úguchuru, arufudabawa
  lun aban Biráü.
Úguchuru gúnfulitu,
Buagu wíchigei wemenigi.
Ferudun bei würibati wadüga,
Ferudun bawa, Wabungiute.
Aganbabei wafurieidun,
Aganbabei wayumuragu,
Ferudun bawa, Baba.
Aganba bei wafurieidun,
Aganba bei wayumuragu,
Ferudun bawa, Baba.

(music p. 61)

Our Holy Mother

Our Holy Mother,
    Show us your way.
Mother of our Lord,
    Fill us with your love.
Mother of our God,
    This is your month to be honored.

Have mercy on us, Guadalupe,
    We are your children, you love us.
Have mercy on us, Blessed Virgin,
    We are your children, we love you.
Have mercy on us, Our Mother,
    We are your children, Our Mother.

Mother, Show Us

Mother, show us
    to your only son.
Holy Mother,
On you we put our trust.
Forgive the bad we have done,
Forgive us, Our God.
Hear our prayers,
Hear our pleas,
Forgive us, our Father.
Hear our prayers,
Hear our pleas,
Forgive us, our Father.

Hilatibu Luagu Gurúa Wawagu Wáguchi

Hilatibu luagu gurúa,
    wawagu Wáguchi,
Suéwaguatibu,
Patarawatibu bigibuagun
    lun wasalubarun,

Héiguatibu ürüwa wéyasu
    lau bugurua.
Wayahubei ladüga wafigoun bun,
Wáguchi, lun wasalubarun.

Béiwatibu, dáwaguatibu
    wadüga, Wáguchi;
Súfuritibu gásügürütibu wawagu
    lun wasalubarun.

Héiguatibu ürüwa wéyasu
    lau bugurua.
Wayahubei ladüga wafigoun bun,
Wáguchi, lun wasalubarun.

(music p. 62)

You Died on the Cross for Us, Our Father

You Died on the Cross
        for Us, Our Father,
They spat on you,
They slapped your face
        for our salvation.

You fell three times
        with your cross.
We cry because of our sins,
Our Father, for our salvation.

You were lashed, You were nailed
        for us, Our Father;
You suffered, You suffered for us
        for our salvation.

You fell three times
        with your cross.
We cry because of our sins,
Our Father, for our salvation.

Saraya Bungiu

Saraya Bungiu,
    Saraya Bungiu,
        Saraya Wabureme.
Gunda hamá sun mutu,
    Gunda hamá sun mutu,
        Gunda ligía me ubou.
Fubei bigarabali le biniwabei wawagu,
Le lánina ibagari.

Madeiru hamutibu María Magdalena
María Salume, lidan bumúaha.
    Saratibu luei ónweni.

Madeiru hamutibu, María Magdalena
María Salume, lidan bumúaha.
    Saratibu luei ónweni.

Ánhelu adeirúbei ñei
Ánhelu adeirúbei ñei
Ligía íchugubei fe
Ligía íchugubei fe

(music p. 64)

God Has Risen

God has risen,
    God has risen,
        Our Lord has risen.
Let everyone be glad,
    Let everyone be glad,
        Let the world rejoice.
Blow your blessed breath on us,
    The breath of life.

Mary Magdalene and Mary Salome,
Did not find you in your tomb.
    You arose from the dead.

Mary Magdalene and Mary Salome
Did not find you in your tomb.
    You arose from the dead.

They found an angel.
They found an angel.
He is the one who told them.
He is the one who told them.

Sian Béheraha Tuma

Sian béheraha tuma bitu
　Tíchawagúniwa bun:
　　Búmari ñou nege la buga.

Sian béheraha tuma bitu
　Tíchawagúniwa bun:
　　Búmari ñou nege la buga

Marihin(ei) bumuti san ligaburi?
Marihin(ei) bumuti san ligaburi?

Nati Joe, ariense ba keimoun woun,
Nati Joe, ariense ba keimoun woun.

(music p.67)

Duña Duña Duña

Duña duña dun, duña duña dun,
　Galali dun, galali dun.

Duña galali, duña galali, luni Pepe Pe.

Duña duña dun, duña duña dun,
　Galali dun, galali dun.

Digala aü, digala aü, digala Pe,
Digala aü, digala aü, digala Pe.

Pepe Pepe Pe, Pepe Pepe Pe,
Pepepe Pe, Pepepe Pe, Peeeeeeee ie!!!

(music p.68)

You Cannot Laugh

You cannot laugh with your sister
> They will say:
>> That she is your girlfriend.

You cannot laugh with your sister
> They will say:
>> That she is your girlfriend.

Don't you see his ways?
Don't you see his ways?

Brother Joe, get ready, let's go.
Brother Joe, get ready, let's go.

Pepe Catches a Fish

Bite again; bite again; bite,
> red snapper bite; red snapper bite.

Bite, red snapper; bite, red snapper, for Pepe Pe.

Bite again; bite again; bite,
> red snapper bite; red snapper bite.

I caught it! I caught it! Pepe caught it!
I caught it! I caught it! Pepe caught it!

Pepe Pepe Pe, Pepe Pepe Pe,
Pepepe Pe, Pepepe Pe, PeeeeeeeeEh!!!

Buiti Binafi

Buite Binafi (cont.)

One Day Tiofila Gone By The Well

One day Ti-o-fila gone by the

well. Suddenly Alba called,"*Nihán aban mafia!*" Ti -

o - fila run *wa- wa guéina*

Keimoun Numa

1. Keimoun numa, numadagunu,   á- lu- ahei Chécheche.
2. Ti-ge-meri   wá-digidigi, li-geme-ri bei á- ra- bu.
3. Tá-lü-dagu   wá-digidigi, la-gú-a- ra ha Chécheche.

1. Keimoun numa numadagunu,   á - lu- a-hei Chécheche.
2. Ti-ge-meri   wádigidigi, li-geme-ri bei á- ra- bu. Ta-
3. Tá-lu-dagu   wádigidigi, la-gú-a- ra ha Chécheche.

1. Keimoun numa numadagunu,   á- lu-a- hei lü- ya- Eh!
2. ru- gounga   wá- digidigi, ligemeri bei   á- ra- bu
3. Tá- lü- da-gu wá- digidigi, lagúara ha   á- ra- bu

1. Keimoun nu- ma lá- ri-gi Che, á- lua-hei numadagunu
2. Keimoun nu- ma lá- ri-gi Che, á- lua-hei numadagunu
3. Keimoun nu- ma lá- ri-gi Che, á- lua-hei numadagunu

1. Keimoun numa, keimoun numa, keimoun numa
2. Keimoun numa, keimoun numa, keimoun numa
3. Keimoun numa, keimoun numa, keimoun numa

Hísienti Sawana Nun

Hí - si- enti sawana nun; Hí- si-

enti duna churunruti le ñei bei nun;

Hí - si-enti fuluri le ñei bei nun;

Hí-sienti hagúaraha gurewegiha ñei baña

nun; tuéi- gien ti - di- bu wewe.

Hísienti Sawana Nun (cont.)

Hí - si-enti lahun - ha duna churunruti

le ñei bei nun; Hí - sienti lahunha garabali

le ñei bei nun; Hí - sienti hagúarahagurewe-

gi ha ñei bañá nun; tu-éi - gien tí- di - bu

wewe.

Mábuiga María

Lúguchu Wabureme

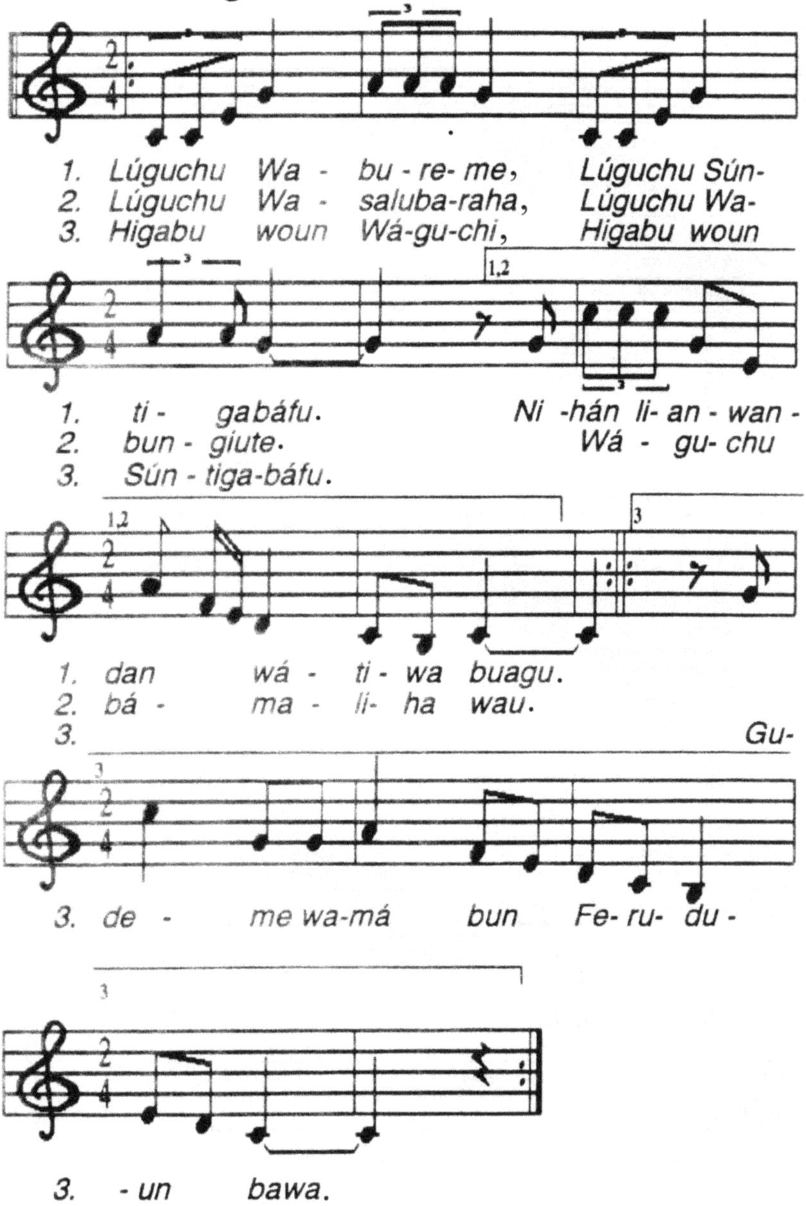

1. Lúguchu Wa - bu - re - me, Lúguchu Sún-
2. Lúguchu Wa - saluba-raha, Lúguchu Wa-
3. Higabu woun Wá-gu-chi, Higabu woun

1. ti - gabáfu. Ni -hán li- an - wan -
2. bun - giute. Wá - gu- chu
3. Sún - tiga-báfu.

1. dan wá - ti - wa buagu.
2. bá - ma - li - ha wau.
3. Gu-

3. de - me wa-má bun Fe- ru- du -

3. - un bawa.

Úguchuru Arufudabáwa

Ú- guchuru, a- rufu-da bawa lun a- ban

Biráü Ú-guchuru gún - fu-litu,

Buagu wíchigei weme - ni-gi. Ferudun

bei würibati wa düga, Ferudun bawa,

Wabungiute. Agan ba-bei wa-furiei -

dun, Agan-babei wa-yu - muragu,

Feru-dun ba- wa, Baba.

Hilatibu Luagu Gurúa Wawagu Wáguchi

Hi-la-ti-bu lu-a-gu gu-rúa

wa-wa-gu, Wá-guchi, Suéwagua tibu, Pa-

tarawatibu bigibuagun lun wasaluba-

run. Heíguatibu ürü- wa wéya-

su lau bugu-rua. Waya-hubei la-

Hilatibu Luagu Gurúa
Wawagu Wáguchi (cont.)

dü- ga wa - figoun bun. Wá-guchi,

Fine

lun wasalu - ba - run. Beíwatibu, Da-

-a waguatibu wadüga, Wáguchi;

Sú-furi- tibu gá - sü- gü - rüti-bu wawa-

D.S. al Fine

gu lun wasalubarun.

Saraya Bungiu

Saraya Bungiu (cont.)

María Magdale- na María Salu- me,

Lidan bumua-ha.   Saratibu Luei ónweni.

Án - he- lu a- dei - rú- bei ñei.

Án - he- lu a- dei- rú- bei ñei.

Ligía íchugubei fe.   Ligía íchugubei fe.

Lubuidu Namule Eyeri

Lu- bui- du na- mule eyeri. Si- si ha - ti

lau uguñe. Lau sun maríengadi la   A-ganba lumuti

nereru lun. Dan le nayarafadu luru-ga bun A-ba lóuaba

hóuniwa.   Wéi - ri - ti lisi - en nun. Namule raü

eyeri, eyeri.

Sian Béheraha Tuma

Si - an béheraha tuma bi- tu tíchawaguniwa

bun: Búma- ri ñou ne- ge la- bu-

ga. Mari - hi - n(ei) bumuti-

sa li - gabu- ri. Mari - hi -

n(ei) bumuti - sa li- ga- bu- ri?

Na- ti Joe, arien-se-ba keimoun woun.

Duña Duña Duña Dun

Duña duña dun, duña duña dun, galali dun, galali

dun.   duña galali, duña galali, luni Pepe Pe.

duña duña dun, duña duña dun, galali dun, galali

dun.   digala aü, digala aü, digala Pe, digala aü, di-

gala aü digala Pe. Pepe Pepe Pe,   Pepe Pepe

Pe, Pepepe Pe, PepepePe, Peeee ei!!!

Editor's Notes for Those Unfamiliar with the Garifuna Language

This book is part of an effort which began in 1972, to reclaim, maintain, and promote the Garifuna culture and language. Mrs. Marcella Lewis is one of the leaders of this effort, being involved in the National Garifuna Council from the very beginning. These efforts are coming to fruition in the publication of several books.

Many years of work by many Garinagu has gone into the preparation of a dictionary spearheaded by Roy Cayetano (The People's Garifuna Dictionary, 1993). This monumental achievement has established a standard, allowing a book such as this to be completed. Sebastian Cayetano has written an excellent book documenting in detail the history, culture and language of the Garinagu in Belize. Felicia Hernandez has written a children's book. A literature is indeed being developed which will facilitate the progress of this rich culture.

The word Garifuna refers to both the language and the person in the singular; it is also an adjective so we can speak of Garifuna people, Garifuna food, Garifuna music, etc. Garinagu is the plural noun, meaning the Garifuna people. The Garinagu have been in Belize since 1802, but the language is among the Arawak group, originating in the Orinoco River area of what is now Venezuela thousands of years ago (Cayetano, 1993). The history of the Garinagu is reflected in their language. The Arawak migrated throughout the islands off the coast of South America over a thousand years ago. The Caribs followed behind and captured Arawak women for wives.

This cultural fusion is demonstrated in an unusual feature of Garifuna, the presence of masculine and common voice. For some meanings there are different words, depending on whether a woman or a man is speaking. The words that only a man uses may come from the Carib language but the rest of the language, including the common voice, is largely derived from an Arawak language. Because this book is written by a woman, it is expressed in the common voice.

Masculine / Common Voice

Meaning	Common Voice	Masculine Voice
woman	hianru	würi
man	eyeri wügúri	
doe	hianru usari	würi usari
come to me	higabu nun	ahü ye
land crab	hürü	wayumu

Normally, the gender of the referent is indicated by the affix, t- (feminine) or l- (masculine). For example:

lúguchu	His mother	túguchu	her mother
luguchi	his father	túguchi	her father
luban	his house	tuban	her house
lilügü ounli	his pet dog	tilügü ounli	her pet dog

The principal, though not the only difference between masculine and common voice lies in the fact that in masculine voice abstract nouns, adverbs and prepositions use the feminine form as can be seen in the following examples:

Meaning	Common Voice	Masculine Voice
foolishness	libidiouníga	tibidiouníga
immediately	guenle	guentó
recently	ligirabuga	tugurabuga
before we arrive	lubaragien wachülürün	tubaragien wachülürün

Even though the use of the masculine voice is on the decline and males can and, for the most part nowadays, do use the common voice, there are certain words having to do with relationships that are strictly reserved for male or female use when they are speaking about their own relationships.

Meaning	Female speech	Male speech
my older brother	nati	níbugaña
my sister-in-law	nigatu	nuguñou
my brother-in-law	nuguñou	nibamu
my mother-in-law	nagürü	nímeidi

Garifuna Grammar

Garifuna grammar is quite complex and very different from Western languages. Nouns, verbs, adjectives, prepositions, and even adverbs, may include person and number designations, usually as a suffix, but sometimes as an affix. For nouns, this is translated as the possessive, but it seems that the meaning reflects an emphasis upon relationship rather than possession.

Root	Person	#	Gender	Garifuna	English
-uma	1st	S		numa	with me
	1st	P		wama	with us
	2nd	S		buma	with you
	2nd	P		huma	with you
	3rd	S	F	tuma	with her
	3rd	S	M	luma	with him
	3rd	P		hama	with them
ichiga	1st	S		níchiga	I give
	1st	P		wíchiga	we give
	2nd	S		bíchiga	you give
	2nd	P		híchiga	you give
	3rdS		F	tíchiga	she gives
	3rd	S	M	líchiga	he gives
	3rd	P		híchiga	they give
Ibagari	1st	S		nibagari	my life
	1st	P		wabagari	our lives
	2nd	S		bibagari	your life
	2nd	P		hibagari	your lives
	3rd	S	F	tibagari	her life
	3rd	S	M	libagari	his life
	3rd	P		habagari	their lives
bibu-	1st	S		bíbutina	I (am) brave
	1st	P		bíbutiwa	we (are) brave
	2nd	S		bíbutibu	you (are) brave
	2nd	P		bíbutiü	you (are) brave
	3rd	S	F	bíbutu	she (is) brave
	3rd	S	M	bíbuti	he (is) brave
	3rd	P		bíbutiun	they are brave

(The meaning of the verb "to be" is included in the adjective.)

-uagu	1st	S		nuágu	on me
	1st	P		wawagu	on us
	2nd	S		buágu	on you
	2nd	P		huágu	on you
	3rd	S	F	tuágu	on her
	3rd	S	M	luágu	on him
	3rd	P		hawagu	on them

Sometimes the root of the verb, deleting the first vowel, is used with suffixes. From Marcela's song, "Hilatibu Luagu Gurúa Wawagu Wáguchu" on page 46, line 4, we see "patarawatibu bigibuagu," meaning "you were slapped on your face."
The following words are used to construct this sentence:

apatara	to slap on the face
-wa	passive voice indicator
-tibu	you (adjectival 2nd person affix)
-igibu	face
bigibu	your face
buágu	on you

Other suffixes and affixes change the meaning of the root word in different ways.

duei	sky
-rügü	in
dueirügü	in the sky
-gien	from
dueigien	from the sky

ekera	to complain
m- or ma-	negative
makera ba	(you) do not complain

gurasu	patience
magurasuni	impatience

ubafu	power
ga-	having the characteristic or ability of
gabafuti	powerful (m)
gabafutu	powerful (f)

Pronunciation

The vowel sounds are like Spanish vowels:

"a" as in "father"
"e" as in "fed"
"i" as the "e" in "scene"
"o" as in "or"
"u" as the "oo" in "good"
"ü" a back unrounded vowel (i.e., the lips are spread when it is produced) that is not used in English.

There are also five nasal vowels corresponding to the oral vowels listed above. These are written as follows:
"an"
"en"
"in"
"on"
"un"
"ün"

Here, the "n", which would usually be followed by a consonant or occur in a word's final position, does not function as a consonant but rather serves to indicate nasality on the preceding vowel.

Consonants are as in English except for the "ñ" which is more like a nasalized "y". The consonants include the following:
/b/ /ch/ /d/ /f/ /g/ /h/ /k/ /l/ /m/ /n/ /ñ/ /p/ /r/ /s/ /t/ /w/ /y/

Stress is usually on the first syllable of two syllable words and the second of longer words. Exceptions to this are marked, using the same conventions as those in the dictionary. Stress is also marked where separation between syllables is not obvious.

Bibliography

Cayetano, E. R. (1992). *Towards a common Garifuna orthography.* Belize: National Garifuna Council.

Cayetano, E. R. (1993). *The People's Garifuna Dictionary: Dimureiágei Garifuna. Garifuna - Inglesi, English - Garifuna.* Belize: National Garifuna Council,

Cayetano, E. R. (1995). *Final report on consultancy on standardization of Garifuna orthography and determining linguistic competence of teachers.* Tegucigalpa, Honduras: Secretaria de Educacion Publica, Proyeto Mejoramiento de la Calidad de la Educacion Basica Subcomponente de Educacion Bilingue Intercultural.

Cayetano, Sebastian (1990, 1993). *Garifuna History, Language, & Culture of Belize, Central America, and the Caribbean,* Revised 1997 with Fabian Cayetano.

Langworthy, Geneva (2002). Language Planning in a Trans-National Speech Community. In: *Indigenous Languages Across the Community,* ed. by Barbara Burnaby and Jon Reyhner. Flagstaff: Northern Arizona University, pp. 41–48.

Palacio, Clifford J. *A Garifuna Vocabulary Compiled in 1666.* <seinebight.com/cjp/caribbean-vocab.htm>

Palacio, Clifford J. *Online Garifuna Lessons.* <seinebight.com/cjp/dir.htm>

Suazo, Salvador (1994). *Conversemos en garífuna* (2nd ed.). Tegucigalpa: Editorial Guaymuras.

www.ingramcontent.com/pod-product-compliance
Lightning Source LLC
Chambersburg PA
CBHW051711040426
42446CB00008B/836